What Kind of Sound?

by Vita Jiménez

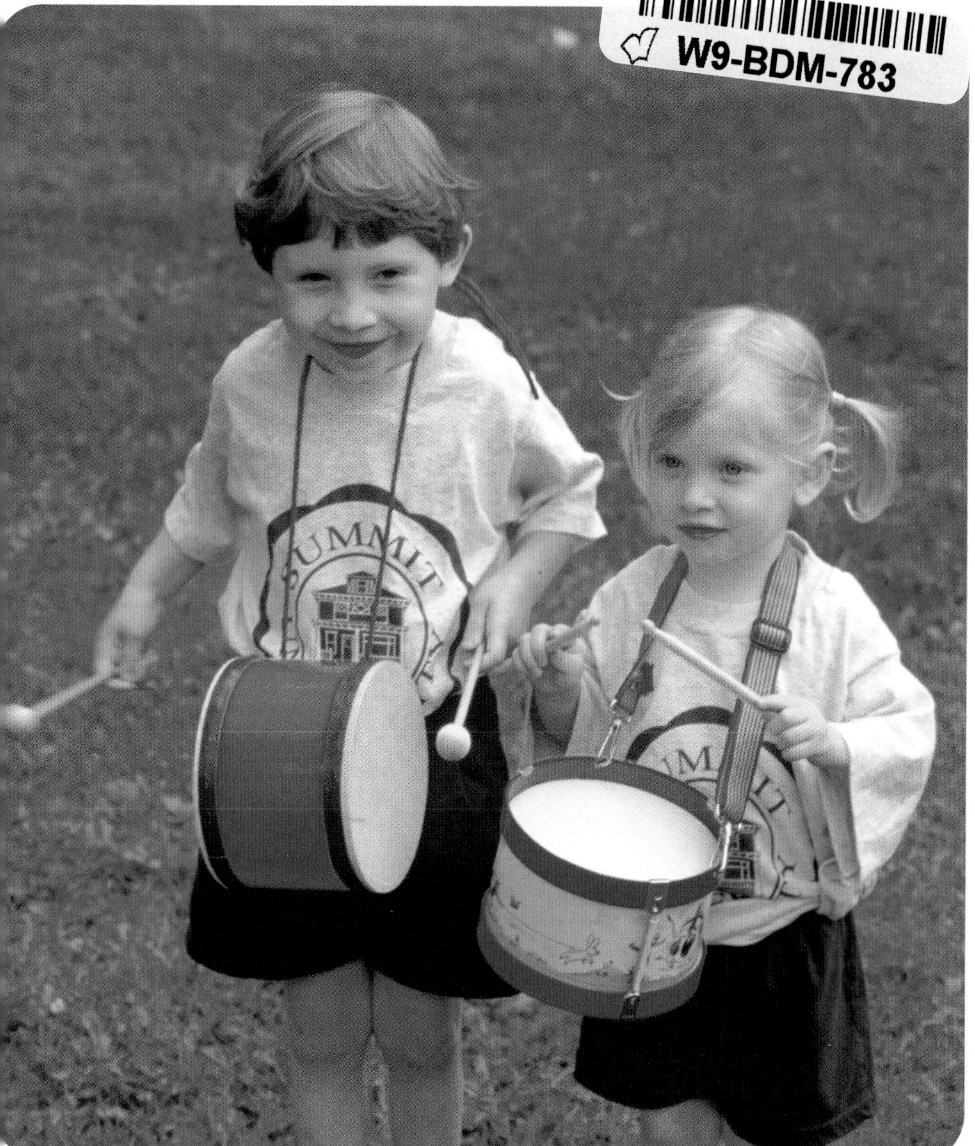

A loud sound.

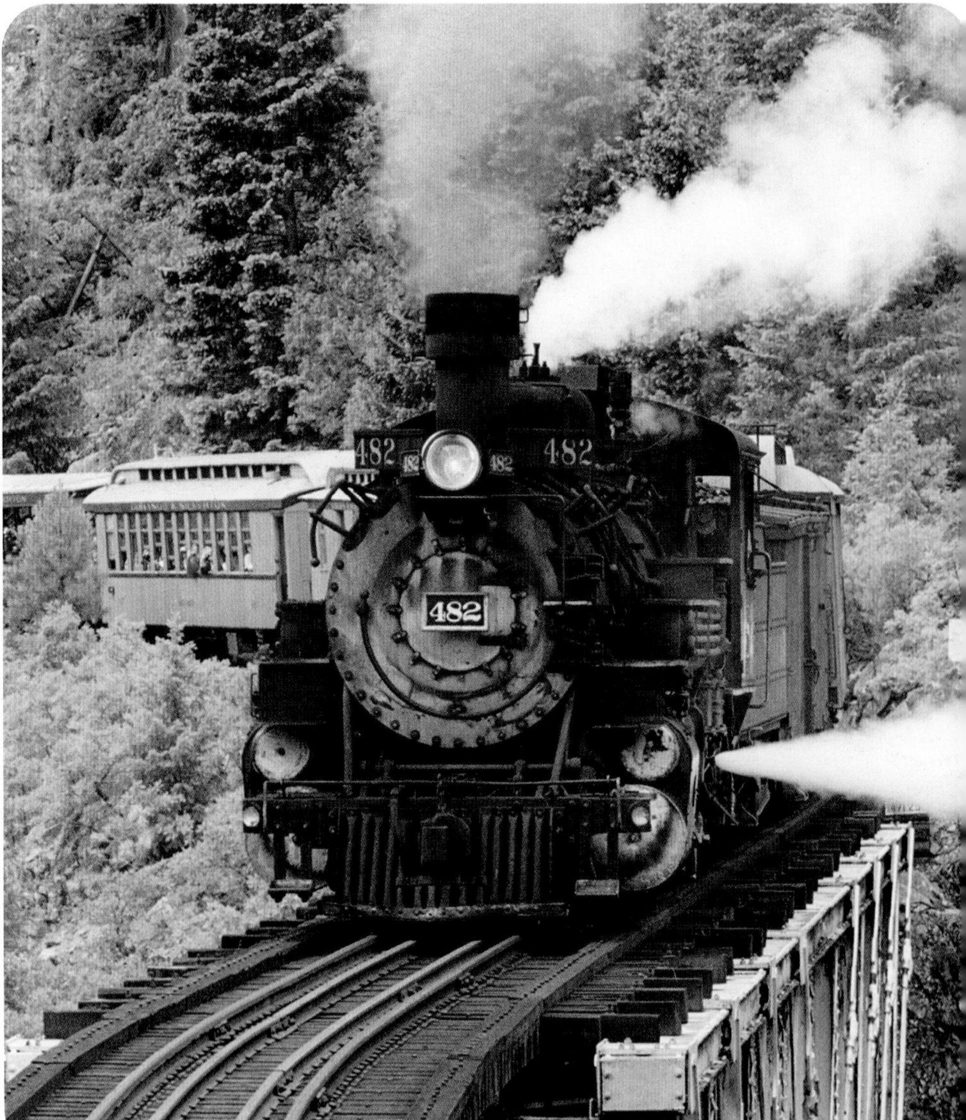

A soft sound.

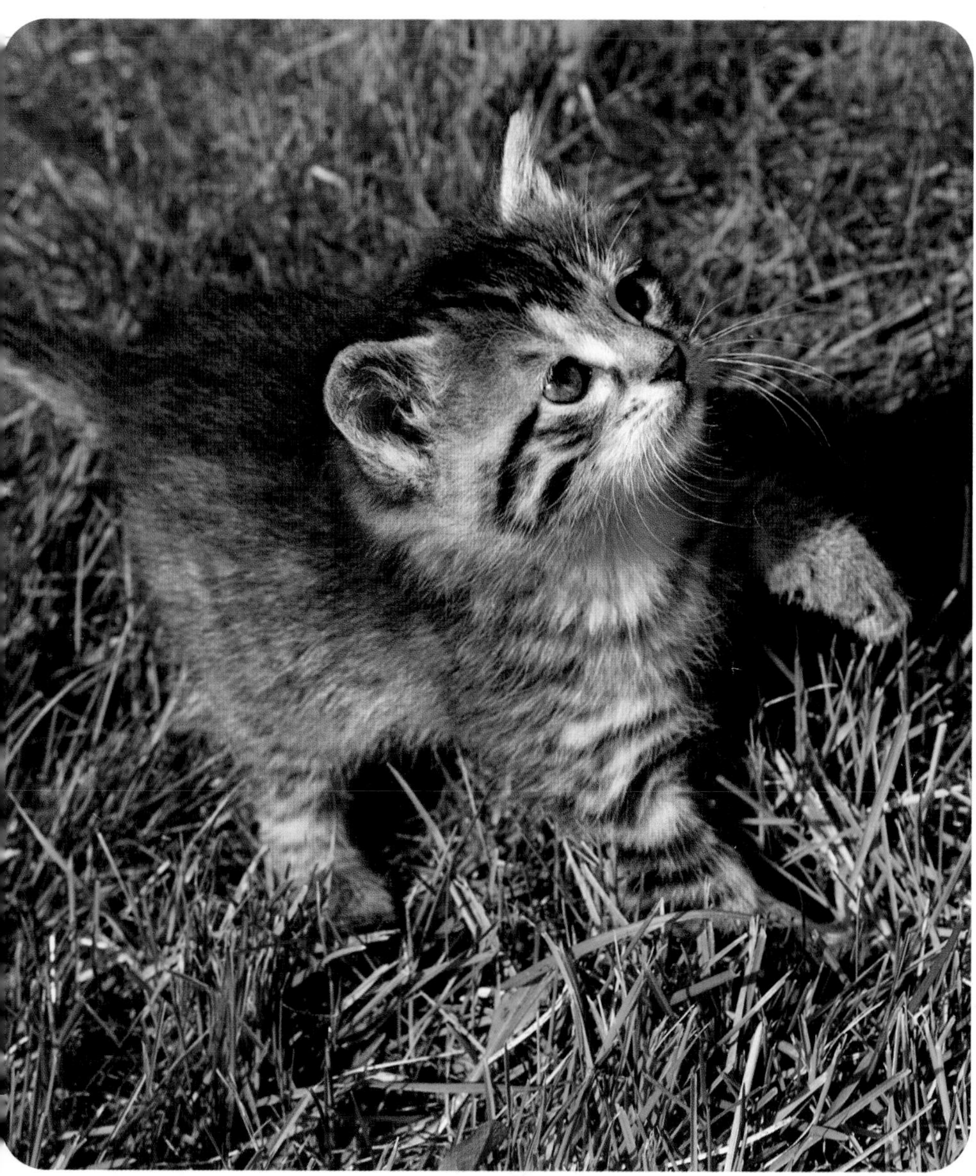

A loud sound.

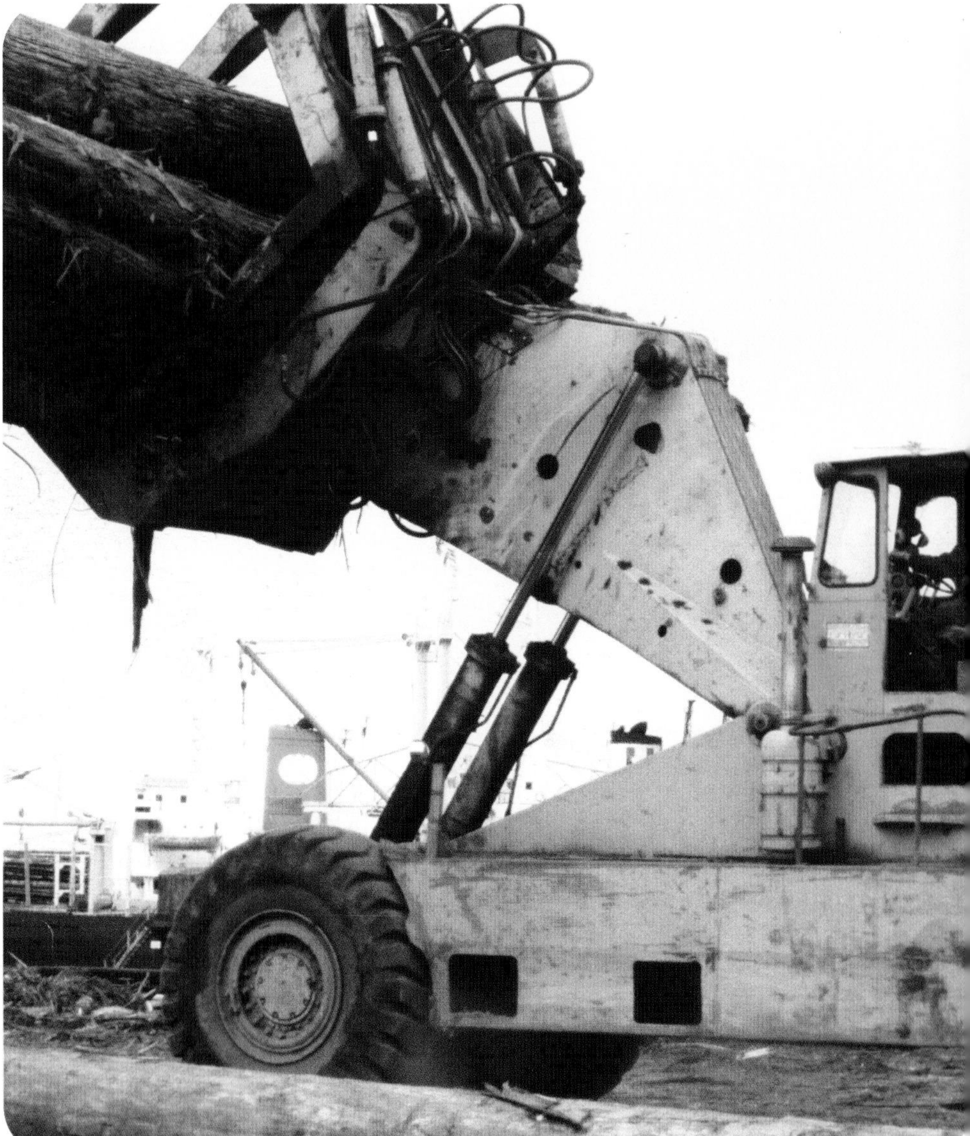

A soft sound.

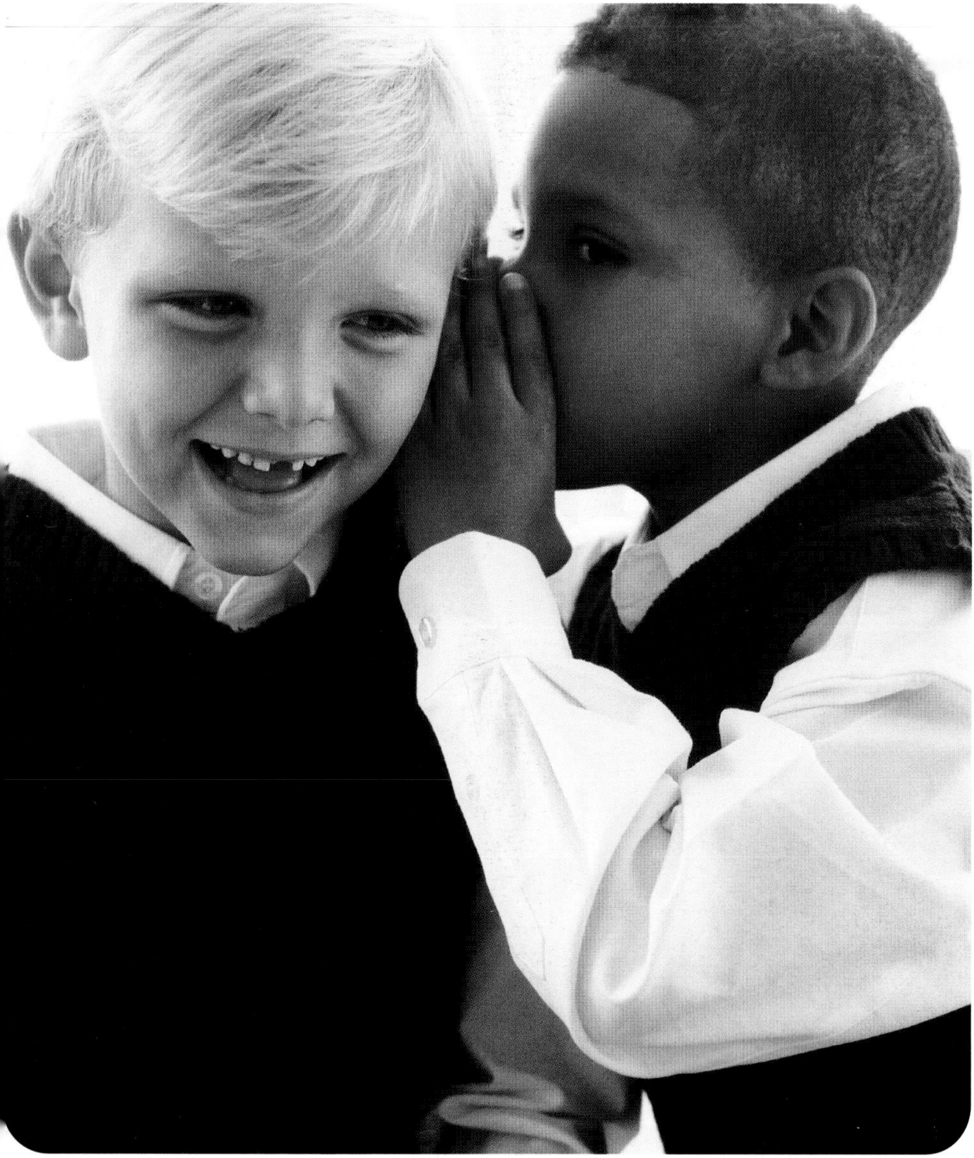

A loud sound.

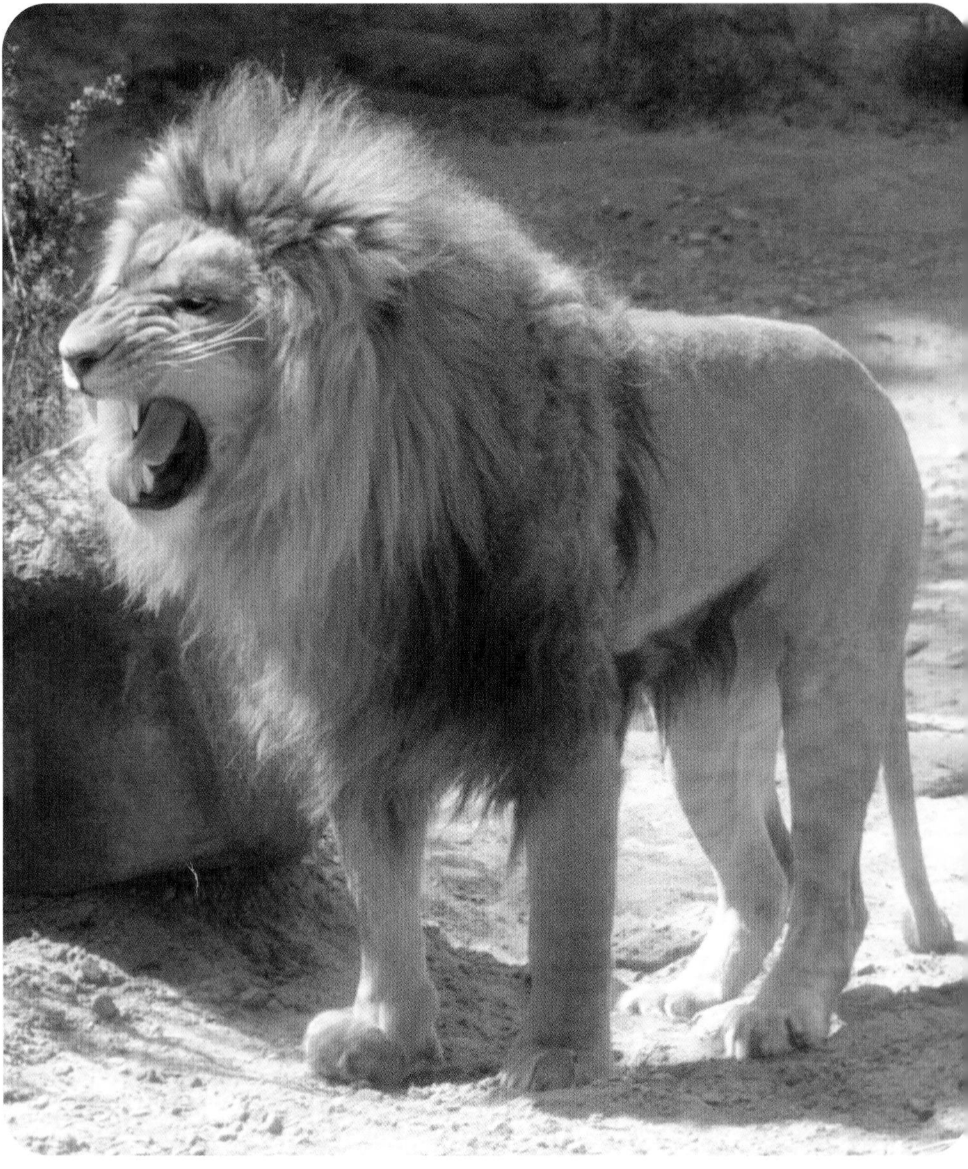

A soft sound.

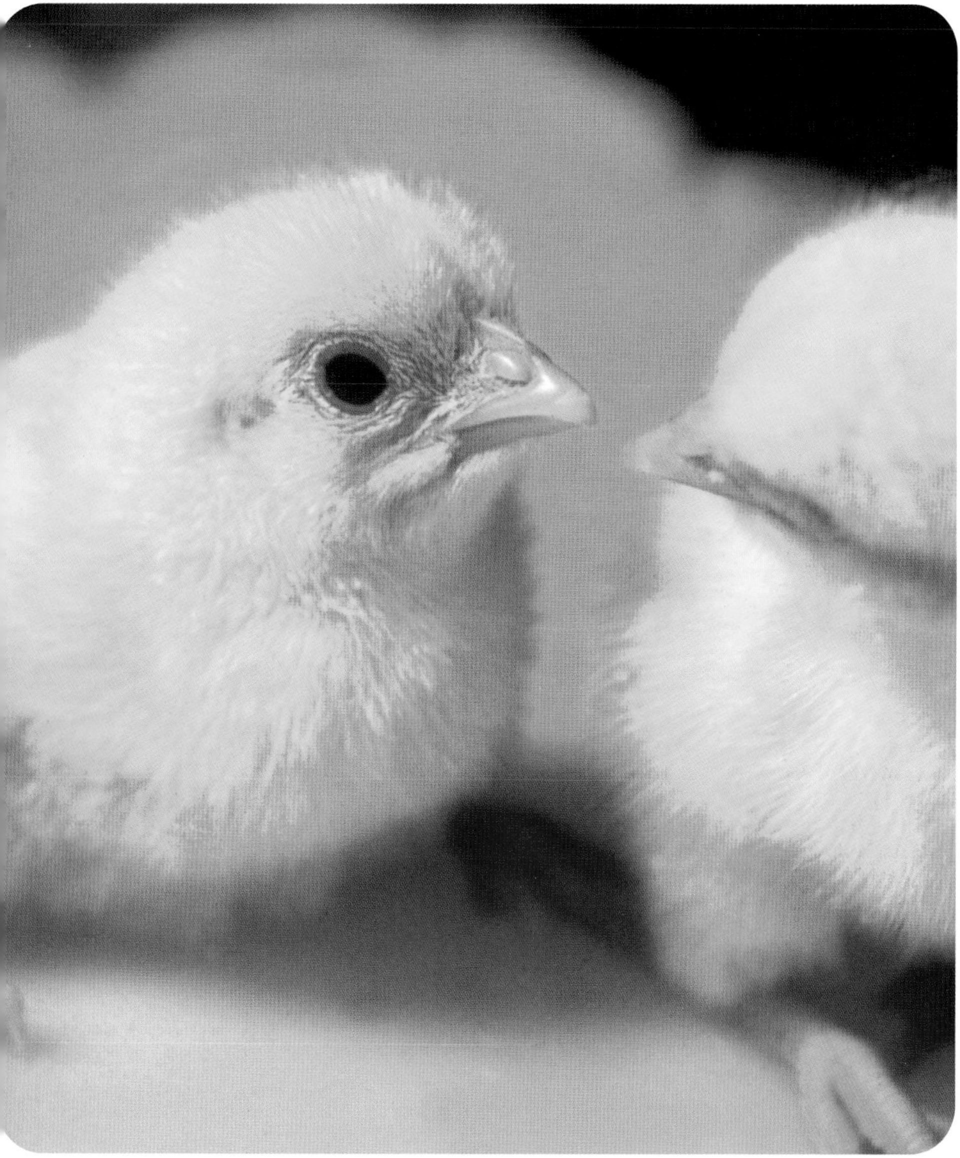

What kind of sounds do you make?

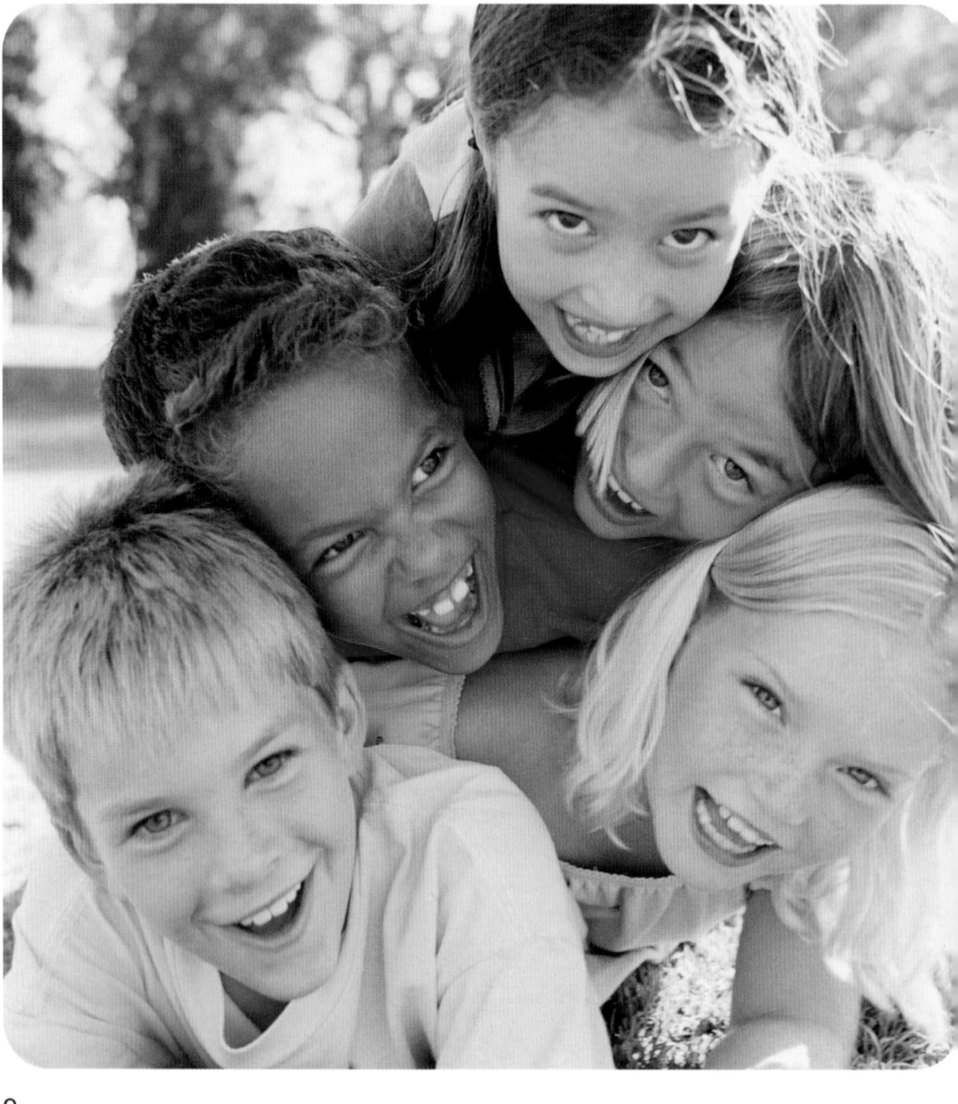